Corvus

Corvus

POEMS BY DANA SONNENSCHEIN

A **wind** CHAPBOOK

Corvus is the 2003 Quentin R. Howard Poetry Prize winner.

Quentin R. Howard founded WIND in 1971 in Pikeville, Kentucky. His goal was to produce an eclectic, high-quality magazine while giving newcomers and emerging writers a chance at publication. For twenty-two years Quentin edited and published the growing magazine from his modest home on an eastern Kentucky hillside overlooking the valley's railroad and coal tipple. During that time WIND became one of the nation's longest-lived and most respected literary journals. And yet, the publication remained one without pretentiousness. Quentin proudly stated, "Readers of WIND include professors, factory workers, and housewives." Throughout the years the work of talented newcomers has appeared in the pages of WIND beside the work of some of the nation's best-known writers.

ISBN 0-9741268-1-0

wind | 90

2003 Quentin R. Howard Poetry Prize judged by
RICHARD TAYLOR.

A native of Louisville, RICHARD TAYLOR is a
professor of English at Kentucky State University
and was appointed Kentucky's Poet Laureate in 1999
for a two year term. He is the author of four
collections of poetry, *Bluegrass, Earthbones, In the
Country of Morning Calm,* and *Stone Eye,* and one
novel, *Girty.* He also wrote the accompanying text
for *The Palisades of the Kentucky River,* a collection of
photographs published by the Nature Conservancy,
and *The Great Crossing: A Historic Journey to the Buffalo
Trace Distillery.* He has been the recipient of two
creative writing fellowships from the National
Endowment for the Arts, as well as an Al Smith
Fellowship in Creative Writing from the Kentucky
Arts Council. He and his wife, Lizz, live near
Frankfort with their three children and own Poor
Richard's Books in historic downtown Frankfort.

Illustrations by HAANS MOTT.
Design by ALEX BROOKS.

WIND
PO Box 24548
Lexington, Ky 40524
www.wind.wind.org

"Dana Sonnenschein has created a compendium of crows. Corbies, black birds, corvus, ravens — these crows fly."
-RICHARD TAYLOR, Judge

"Like a priest lifting communion to a world sieved by terror, Dana Sonnenschein offers poems that urge us to 'Listen,' because 'The gift returns to the giver, many times over.' Weaving together history and legend, her poems allow us to enter the world through sensual detail ... yet they also ask us to give up our eyes ... to trust our ears in order to understand what separates people and what binds them together ...to hear the cry of a raven and a crow 'come calling caw, ka, baraka, om, ah.' An intense and compelling collection, Corvus reminds us why we need to be quiet, to listen, even to a world that threatens to drown out the call of birds."
-VIVIAN SHIPLEY, Crazy Quilt

Contents

Crows and ravens, all in the genus Corvus ... have very large vocal repertoires, including loud and harsh territorial calls and predator alams, and softer, often more musical notes used in close quarters for communication with a mate or family member. Many species on occasion make rattling noises or even clear bell-like notes ... Crows and ravens can mimic human speech, although they rarely do so in the wild.

Someone has predicted that when man, through his ingenuity, has finally destroyed all his neighbors and himself too, there will still be Crows ...

I

IN THE NORTH WOODS

Listen, in the north woods, any unnamable sound may be a raven, and the quiet is a secret in its keeping. That shadow, that shifting in the periphery of vision may be a raven. Or blood. All birds are black, crossing the sun. How will you know? The raven sometimes flies as the crow flies but fans its tail into a black diamond, writes in the snow, picks out the eyes, rises like memory and twists and dives like thought, mercurial. In one account, he cracks the shell that carried us into this world and leaves us to our own devices. Another says that she returns, leading wolves who will break open the body, the dark chest and the chambers of the heart. Listen, they speak in tongues.

II

How Can You Tell a Raven from a Crow?

One right after the other, two black birds flash over
the heath and under the green canopy, fold their
wings, and settle on a branch. It's a matter of scale:
The crow takes one end of the branch and the raven,
the other; the raven, hammer-headed, hunched and
massy, is easily twice the crow's size. Slick and
apparently unruffled, the crow holds white bread,
tears it to bits, and flings his head back, swallowing.
Raven hops sideways, hoping to tilt things in his
favor. Cousin, he croaks, coming closer, cousin.
Crow flies off, caws echoing.

III

Corvus corax at the White Tower

Running after a raven, a girl calls out, "I always talk
to them. I heard if you talk to them, they talk back."
Her friend laughs. The raven in the green leg band
clicks its tongue, cocks its head at me, leans to the
stonework and clicks again. Because of a prophecy
that England will last as long as ravens roost at the
White Tower, men in red coats keep six ravens with
their primaries clipped – they can fly, but they can't
fly too far. As if you could improve the odds by
making the place a zoo. We only have the day here,
but I think I have come four thousand miles to see
two ravens with their heads ruffled up, bowing to
one another, and how, when one takes the other's
beak in its own, they hold each other perfectly still.
Around the corner, one raven is in molt; still another
tears at tree bark, sharpening its aim, its hooks. A
third perches on wrought iron by my side as if to
take me under its wing: it has the blackest eye I've
ever seen, and the feathers on top of its bill move
although there is no wind. It could be seven minutes
or seven years I'm standing there, hearing voices
rise and fall around me; when I leave, I know that,
at a certain time each afternoon, the ravens roll
bloody knucklebones. Like runes.

IV

Shadow of a Shadow

The rune of claw-mark in the snow we bend to read: death fell from the sky, the shadow of a shadow, in this valley in the Adirondacks. For the raven has not returned to Noah's hand but still flies to and fro above the earth, summering north and wintering south, staking his claim and claiming his right. Each wing-tip incises eternity on the heavens: a black angel's figure-eight. Perhaps he will leave us something. A testament, say, words in a dead language or a vole's skull nested in bones curled and crushed, the cast of a raven's gullet. As we cross through hemlocks and yellow birch, I hear the raven's quork, that rock spiral made sound. When I call out, nothing answers. When I raise a hand to block the sun, the gesture becomes a warding off or an invitation, my wrist, a place to land. The raven circles above us, folds its wings, and dives with a cry, only to soar up again. At the last minute, we hold nothing.

V

Cemetery Angel

Anything raised to the first power is itself. Thus, the black angel, beautiful and shining as a crow, perpetual, our lady hovering at the edge of vision, our teacher at the threshold of memory. When you look, she isn't there, only the hushing of wings, only sleeves of stone, blank eyes. If she is the angel of death, she knows that the squirrel's eye weeps as it decays by the roadside, and the body sinks into itself, returning to Platonic form, chalk outline, diagram on the blackboard. She knows, too, that skin becomes leather and the tensile strength of tendon and sinew, the usefulness of bone: scapula for hoe and rib for awl. She scatters vertebrae like beads. Look, she says. As a crow looks for corn, as a crow listens for worms. She turns as if to write upon the sky: carbon-based life form, coal frosted with ash, cinders bright and cold after rain. You will be tested. When you stare into the fire, you will see a tree of light, and you will be burning, burning. This smoke is omnipresent but invisible, she says. The children may hold their breath as they walk past the graveyard, but they know. They throw themselves on their backs in the snow and flap their arms. Angels begin in shadow.

VI

Odin's Ravens

Memory said, More. Thought said, Never.

Memory said, Never. Thought said, More.

Thought said, Never. Memory said, More.

Thought said, More. Memory said, Never.

VII

A Murder of Ravens

Like harbingers, the warriors mark each other with
their bright swords, and their bodies open into the
other world. We always come, like the wolf, for
our own, when they have thrust and stabbed, hewn
and hacked: Morrigan, Medb, and Badb, Cuchulain's
god-mothers, knocking and bowing like three
ravens. And we are feared, for we eat the dead and
we eat the living, and when men come searching
for blade and ring, for someone they know or love,
they no longer recognize what they find as what
they made. The kingdom. The glory. The light in the
raven's eye that shines like a mirror. One, two, three,
and then so many ravens: as if a cloud covered the
battlefield, a shadow like bad faith or bad blood. A
murder of ravens.

VIII

THE CORBIES' BONE

Ah, ah, the corbies' bone, where is the corbies' bone
cast into the boughs? Follow the night's road. Follow
the corbies' road, slick and black and rushing out
of the hills, eyegleams between the caution yellows,
and something dashes – Roadkill, they like to call it.
Ah, ah. People run down anything that tries to cross
them.

IX

Impact Study

ELS: I-91, I-95. In America, crow populations appear to be thriving, as morning commuters along the Eastern Corridor can attest. MS: Crows strutting on the median and shoulder, crows perched in a row on a lamppost, appearing to bow over traffic; finally, CU: a single crow hunched on a branch at roadside, cawing. Decrease traffic noise, bringing up bird track until it's startlingly loud for the CU. LS: A family group flies out in the early light to hunt for stricken deer and small game, the splatter and smear we leave behind as fast as we can, bodies tumbled and flung to the roadside. Crows see sharp. By rush hour this morning, the family has claimed a doe along I-91 and gone to work. Look. Cut to CU: deer. Crows need not go for the eyes with their dull knives. Not when the hind is opened according to the huntsman's old art, breast and belly riven. CU: medieval woodcut. LS: Zoom in to MS where a crow rises above the whitetail's flank, pulling a string of gut that hums as if the body were electric. Cut to CU. The others call, harping, harping their one note.

X

Raven Songs

… Vaulted and framed in gold, the hall stood high, and the guest in it slept until the black raven, blithe-hearted, sang heaven's joy. Then the brightness came to pass, shining after shadows.

… And the father began to recite, sang mournfully that his son hangs to bring joy to the raven, and he, old and wise, may not help him any further.

… Nor shall the harp's song awaken the warriors, but the dark raven, hastening over those doomed to die, many-voiced, telling the eagle how he flew to break his fast. Then the raven with the wolf shall reave the slain.

XI

RAVEN GAMES

Getting a raven to sense a trap, that takes learning.
The young watch others eat and don't forget: any
body may be playing dead, so it's one step forward,
two hops back. The Inuit call, Tagaluk, Tagaluk. Tag,
you're it. Raven points to Caribou, comes back later.
It's luck the first time. Now, plucking at an Eagle's
tail, grabbing a Wolf's gray plume — shadow me,
king of the tree, all that flap — no one has to teach
them that. Raven games. Hang by this foot, hang by
that, hang by your bill like an acrobat. Break off a
stick, dig up a stone, pace off the ground around
this bone. Roll down the sky, bathe in the snow,
make it up as you go.

XII

Genesis

When spring comes in a red mist, crows bring sticks
for the nest. They brood. Come summer, some have
a taste for green apples, hold fruit against bark, and
augur for the worm. Where toads secrete the poison
of their fear, crows turn them inside-out to eat, and
here, along the lakeshore, a family of fish crows
hunts for freshwater snails, leaves a shellheap beneath
their favorite perch.

On one tropical island, the crow clans make three
tools to gather insects: straight, bent, and hooked.
Look, no hands! They take a bird's eye view, grip
with claws, trim with beaks, cache their artifacts of
twigs and leaves near where they roost. Head tilted
to one side, jaws clamped on a stem, they pick the
locks of trees and pass their knowledge on. It's show
and tell time in the garden.

XIII

Indian Giver

Listen. In the Northeast, the People still have the story of how Crow brought corn. In a world where there was no word for time, Crow saw it growing in the Creator's garden, and it was good. So Crow flew North, carrying seeds in his craw, seeds the color of sky, blood, and sun. He clawed up a heap, a hole to plant them in. So the People built mounds for *Teosinte*, First Corn, to grow upon, and they kept the best seeds to plant again. Over many summers, the People made *Teosinte* maize. They made it Indian corn. Maybe Crow gave corn to this People knowing they would give it back many-fold, willy nilly, no matter how many stones they cast to keep his kind out of their gardens. Nowadays, the Pequots tell this story in a museum, and I carry it out with me. Maybe I take it so I will not starve. Maybe I am like the English who dug up and stole baskets of corn when they landed on Cape Cod. Or maybe the story is meant for me, for anyone who listens. Crow is still hunter and gatherer, benefactor, malefactor, Indian giver. Listen to his calling. The gift returns to the giver, many times over.

XIV

The Cursing of the Birds

As they scratched side by side in the clearing,
Dove asked, "Who is the most beautiful bird in all
Africa?" Guinea Fowl and Francolin and the other
birds answered,

> The blacker the berry, the sweeter the juice,
> Raven is more beautiful than me and you.

The black bird flew down from where she
watched, from where he perched, like a shadow
from which all colors run, like the shadow to
which they return. When she saw him, Dove
asked for a potion so that they would be alike.
Raven promised to meet them all the next day but
one and, while the other birds watched, ran his
claw around Dove's throat, giving her the neck-
ring she still wears.

Then the other birds asked to be made like Raven.
"What will you give me in return?" asked Raven.
"You can do whatever you want to us so that we
will be like you," they said, imagining witch
bracelets and warrior marks. "You shall be
changed," said Raven.

The next day but one, Raven bowed her shining
head and clicked at Guinea Fowl, pecking the
termites' tower: "Unclean." And Raven clucked,
"Unclever," at Francolin, clawing among the
sheaves:

    All that you claim is mine,
    & I will say what will be thine.
    Spots for Guinea Fowl like Leopard's pain,
    Red mouth for Francolin who steals the grain.

And Raven turned to the other birds and flapped
in their faces:

    I curse you by the straight and crooked,
    Tooth, claw, snare and cook-pot.
    Let all the birds learn truth from one
    Who speaks like me with double tongue.

XV

GATE OF THE CROW

Meat gods in molt, black as Nut, living crows line
the Heit el-Ghorab at Giza. South of the Wall,
brewery, bakery, butchery, the business of life in
the Old Kingdom; north of the Wall, three great
pyramids and many mastabas, each with dishes,
statuettes, a false door for the spirit to fly through
at twilight. In this life, all must pass through the
Gate of the Crow. In the afterlife, it is written,
you must walk through the Wall to find Judgment
in the West. You must speak the name of each
gatekeeper as you pass and utter your heart at last,
for if it balance Ma'at's feather — no more than
truth, no less than harmony — you shall be blessed;
you shall live in eternal form.

You can still see where the workers carved
limestone along red lines, how artists blocked in
ideal pharaohs and queens as if they'd dipped a
finger in the blood of the living. Make good your
dwelling in the graveyard, the archaeologists
translate. Like overseers, they sort and tally
fragments — copper chisels, faience beads and
fish-bones, clay seals — while terra cotta workers
come to life at a word and carry baskets of dust
and grave goods beneath the Gate's lintels. Of

course, they do not believe in *ka*, the spirit that
rises, new-feathered – when you are dead – as *ba*,
the bird with your face, or *akh*, your echo pale as
breath. Nowadays no one knows the names of
the gatekeepers, the syllable that is key and
keyhole. *Ka*, the crows say. Black and still as
canopic jars, they click their tongues and chorus,
We are the cause and the way, full of awe and
offal – make good your dwelling, for you will be
called to account. Again, you will meet gods.

XVI

Ideogram

Lift your face. Close your eyes to see the spirit of
the sun, red in black, a crow rising, a crow walking
across the sky, your life, a crow that marks what has
been. Touching the temple, the brush of wings.

XVII

Wisdom

Give up your eye, and it will come. The ravens whet
their beaks on branches of ash.

XVIII

On Natural Selection

Light on such black wings makes them shine bright and inexorable as glacier ice, so that the raven, hovering over the nests of smaller birds, looks like an angel of natural selection. When the wind blows, the cradle will rock. It's a matter of pressures. Ravens have a corner on this wood, uphold this stretch of the heavens, have found a niche. They nest late in winter. A risk. But time gives them an edge: the thrush's nest is like a basket of Easter eggs for the foraging mother. How delicately she carries an egg, knowing what it holds. Her mate unweaves the stick-and-grass house of the magpies and takes their new fledglings to feed his own. Inside, the young ravens' mouths are pale. Ravenous, ravening. Those large eyes fill their heads with darkness, trembling and reflective.

The world has such a hunger for life.

XIX

Lost in Translation

Crows congregate on our Connecticut hilltop come morning, their call and response something like triangulating, only there are more than three crows, and they weave through the trees so that a pattern of moving sound passes around and through where we sit, on Sunday with our coffee, quietly. Each *caw* is cognate, as far as we can tell; sometimes one bird conjugates or inflects the root word as if it were Latin and not an older idiom. *Cave corvum.* Or maybe they are searching for a tone, their *caw, caw* and *caw caw* echoing between *guffaw* and an exaggerated, knowing, not unsympathetic *aw.* But what they intend – and what they mean to one another – may be without the irony we hear more with each repetition. *Come, come* or *all, I'll, awl,* they seem to call. Does their foreign and familiar tongue create the ambiguity we hear? Perhaps they came to greet the sun. By ones and twos, they glide silently over the clearing where we live, understanding all things imperfectly.

XX

A Raven's Tale

One morning a raven comes, curious, perhaps, about the crows' calling. I hear its wings working the air, glimpse them closing like two shadow-hands against the wall of the sky as it lands in the top of an oak. Then it begins to talk: sounds like a baby wawling, gurgling, then a deeper voice, the tones changing as the raven carries on a conversation I hear as if it came from a further room, one voice become two, someone reading a story, or part of a dream, two voices become one. No wonder the English once thought these birds conceived by billing, bore their young by mouth: their dark issue, their words. This raven's tale is no story I know. The door opens a crack, the crows drift off like burnt paper caught in a draft, and still the raven speaks, hopping deliberately from branch to branch until all I can see is a green shaking — as if the woods had stretched and ruffled its leaves. What does the raven claim? All that lies within these bounds? When I tiptoe closer to hear, a shadow unclasps and flies away.

The next morning, I wake as usual to dogs barking across the road, and then for once I hear someone calling to them, "Come on, calm down, calm down now," and the dogs go still. "Calm, calm," says the voice from the trees.

XXI

Crow Calling

When you are counting on crows, one is for sorrow,
two for mirth, three for a wedding, four for a birth.

The village crow, its tongue cut by boys, torments
the crone, calling her name all day long. When
someone's child finds a feather by the chimney, the
old woman says, Looks singed, don't pick that up:
Crow pays his tribute to the devil with feathers.
What's he get? You know what they say. Crow on
the thatch, death soon lifts the latch. Ha, ha.

Back in the day, it was lucky to find a dead crow on
the road. Now it means another virus. Ominous.
Sure, crows still glean in the corn, one to watch, one
to warn. They have bones to pick with us: the crow
nailed up on a fencepost to scare off the rest, the
roosts emptied with a shotgun blast. Small wonder
they leave us in the coming dark. See how the crows
make wing toward the woods, the flock's four-
dimensional geometry intuitive and complete, a
curve that could become anything. Oh Crow, read
as a sign, Crow named as if you were one word,
our *Corvus brachyrhynchus*, one crow out of many,
caurinus, ossifragus, imparatus et alia, world without end.
Crow, come home to roost. Crow, come, calling
caw, *ka, baraka, om*, ah, a

Printed in the United States
1044300006B/127-489

THE TRINKET POEMS

THE TRINKET POEMS
ANN FISHER-WIRTH

a *wznd* chapbook

Illustrations by Haans Mott.
Design by Alex Brooks.

WIND
PO Box 24548
Lexington, Ky 40524
www.wind.wind.org

ISBN 0-9741268-1-0

The Trinket Poems is the 2003 Quentin R. Howard Poetry Prize runner-up.

Quentin R. Howard founded WIND in 1971 in Pikeville, Kentucky. His goal was to produce an eclectic, high-quality magazine while giving newcomers and emerging writers a chance at publication. For twenty-two years Quentin edited and published the growing magazine from his modest home on an eastern Kentucky hillside overlooking the valley's railroad and coal tipple. During that time WIND became one of the nation's longest-lived and most respected literary journals. And yet, the publication remained one without pretentiousness. Quentin proudly stated, "Readers of WIND include professors, factory workers, and housewives." Throughout the years the work of talented newcomers has appeared in the pages of WIND beside the work of some of the nation's best-known writers.

2003 Quentin R. Howard Poetry Prize judged by Richard Taylor.

A native of Louisville, Richard Taylor is a professor of English at Kentucky State University and was appointed Kentucky's Poet Laureate in 1999 for a two year term. He is the author of four collections of poetry, *Bluegrass, Earthbones, In the Country of Morning Calm,* and *Stone Eye,* and one novel, *Girty.* He also wrote the accompanying text for *The Palisades of the Kentucky River,* a collection of photographs published by the Nature Conservancy, and *The Great Crossing: A Historic Journey to the Buffalo Trace Distillery.* He has been the recipient of two creative writing fellowships from the National Endowment for the Arts, as well as an Al Smith Fellowship in Creative Writing from the Kentucky Arts Council. He and his wife, Lizz, live near Frankfort with their three children and own Poor Richard's Books in historic downtown Frankfort.

"'What space for the sacred in this century?' Ann Fisher-Wirth asks in her remarkable *The Trinket Poems*. This collection both investigates possible answers and becomes a kind of answer in itself for, having read it, one feels as if one has encountered the sacred. The poems trace the author's transformation into the character of Trinket from Tennessee William's *The Mutilated*. The role-playing allows her to explore our big themes – history and aging and hunger and depravity and redemption – always in startling and courageous language. She takes us to a room 'full of gods and sailors' with 'Mardi Gras beads looped over the mirror,' and when the play is over we emerge reluctantly, dazzled and enlightened by what we have seen."

–Beth Ann Fennelly, *Open House* and *Tender Hooks*

"Precise and fast, sexy and humane, blending the illusions of theater and the realities of everyday life – or is it the reality of theater and the illusions of everyday life? – *The Trinket Poems* are all about survival: the unglamorous, ordinary, difficult kind, where people go on because they have to. Fisher-Wirth offers a vision of what's ugly, what's beautiful and what's simply and inescapably factual."

–Daisy Fried, *She Didn't Mean to Do It*

"*The Trinket Poems* speak from an intimate stage where poet, performer, and woman tangle. Ann Fisher-Wirth produces these poems right out of the stage's bric-a-brac, discovering in the impermanence of sets and roles the foul rag-and-bone shop of the womb and heart. Although Tennessee Williams' Trinket is no poet, Ann Fisher-Wirth could not have written this half-real, half-theatrical, abjectly human sequence without her. These lush poems capture liminal spaces between stage and page, performance and desire, youth and age. In their insouciant ownership of and mourning for female sexuality, they are unique."

–Mairéad Byrne, *Nelson & the Huruburu Bird*

"In *The Trinket Poems*, Ann Fisher-Wirth explores the boundaries between reality and illusion, between pain and joy, between youth and age, between life and death, and finds them veil-thin. Original in subject, powerful in theme and depth, compelling in its underlying narrative line, *The Trinket Poems* is one of the best chapbooks I've ever read. I could NOT put it down."

–Patricia Fargnoli, *Necessary Light*

Contents

*In the earliest tragedy Dionysos was not actually present but merely imagined . . .
Later an attempt was made to demonstrate the god as real and to bring the
visionary figure, together with the transfiguring frame, vividly before the eyes of every
spectator.*

Friedrich Nietzsche, *The Birth of Tragedy*

They are the same gods they always were, but fallen.

William Carlos Williams, *Kora in Hell*

Preface

By Michele Cuomo

"The Mutilated" was first presented as part of a double bill entitled *Slapstick Tragedy*. It opened at the Longacre Theatre on February 22, 1966, and closed after only seven performances. Its author, Tennessee Williams, described it as "a wildly idiomatic sort of tragedy," but Stanley Kauffman's opening night *New York Times* review saw no evidence of transcendence in the work, just a drunken vision, a "glandular and alcoholic religiosity."

In April 2002 I directed a production of *The Slapstick Tragedy* at the University of Mississippi, featuring Ann Fisher-Wirth as Trinket Dugan in *The Mutilated*. The cast truly found the story when they rehearsed the entire piece with the sound, movement, and spirit of hungry animals.

Trinket's left breast has been removed. Her mutilation leaves her heart close to the surface. Celeste, her shoplifting prostitute companion, "exposes" Trinket's mutilation, not only by scratching it on the bathroom wall, but also by slowly opening her heart. Trinket at first seeks to salve her wound with "the Christmas gift of a lover." In our production, Trinket adorned herself with Mardi Gras beads and stretched them out to her drunken sailor, offering herself as a sacrifice in a Dionysian ritual; she returned to the spirit of the original Mardi Gras carnival, a valediction to *carne*, offering herself to indulge the sailor's desire to rend her further. This ritual, however, is a failure, as the sailor and Trinket tear away from each other when Celeste's screams interrupt them, and the sailor falls asleep. Trinket is then stirred by maternal longings, and mourns her missing breast for its ability to nourish. She transfers her desire back to the maternal, and feeds and comforts the starving, childlike Celeste. She passes wine and wafer to Celeste, and in that ritual of the mass, her room at the Silver Dollar Hotel becomes a sacred space where Trinket and Celeste can commune with the divine.

Butoh, the subject of the final poem in the series, was born out of a reaction against the devastation of Hiroshima and Nagasaki. The butoh dancer seeks to commune with the dead and suffering, to take

the body to a crisis point, which then allows the dance to become a meditation on the body and the spirit. It is a dance form with roots in theatre traditions; theorist Antonin Artaud and actor/director Jean Louis Barrault influenced its founders. It also borrows from traditional Japanese performance styles to contextualize body, time, and space.

Tatsumi Hijikata pioneered the butoh movement in the 1950s, with early works that were often overtly sexual and violent. The 1970s standard use of white makeup and conscious application of Japanese performance styles added more lyrical elements to butoh expression. Regardless of the period, however, butoh movement mixes the material and the spirit, in a choreographic approach that Shizune Tomoe calls "Toforri," relying not only on visual energy, but also on energy flow. For instance, a dancer finding "The Bird," a movement sequence by Min Tanaka, seeks to embody the spirit of Bird, to discover its nature through the dance, "to live the question of life and death" (Tomoe).

Have we become so mutilated, have we amputated spirit from our daily existence, or are we ready to become butoh artists, moving our bodies and spirits as one? Can we see the most sacred moments in the most profane spaces? Can we see the beauty in "glandular and alcoholic religiosity"? Tennessee Williams in *The Mutilated* celebrates what Ann Fisher-Wirth has named "the holy whore." *The Trinket Poems* invite us to join him in this celebration.

Kauffmann, Stanley. "Tennessee Williams Returns." The New York
    Times. Wednesday, February 23, 1966.

Tomoe, Shizune. http://www.tomoe.com/contents/aboutbutoh_e.html

Williams, Tennessee. "Preface to Slapstick Tragedy." Esquire. August 1965.

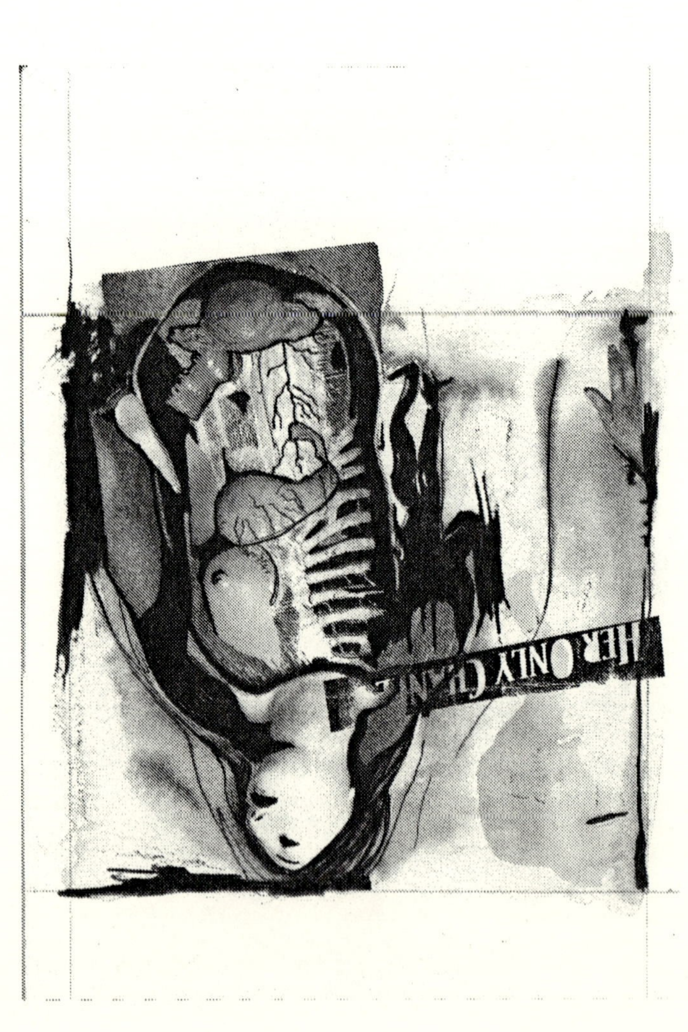
HER ONLY GLANCE

After Many Years She Returns to the Stage
in a Play by Tennessee Williams

"It is a dream! I want it to go on."
Nietzsche, The Birth of Tragedy

She runs her fingers over the cheek and down the throat
and slender chest of this boy, fuck age-appropriate
fuck that she's a professor it's not specific to him anyway
she arches her body against him and moans
when he orders her be my slave and God she has
climbed inside delirium
                              between scenes she
sits by herself in the theatre envying the students
like a pack of puppies with each other's bodies
last time they made love her husband
whispered to her holding her close
her face in his hands   *throat   wrist   breast*
reminded her of her magic words as a child
for the white meat where the blood beat close to the surface
to shame her

                Why did she give it up

Why did she let it stop

It's 1964 she's
passing the white-flowered bushes in front of Little Bridges
that accost her with their wild sweet rotting meat smell
night and joy she is big strides
coming in tights from the improv group
where everyone sleeps with everyone sooner or later
and so why not touch   caress
let the audience watch
them burn   lithe arcs and turns   oh foolish

bound by the body and wanting to be fire
in the dance she
throws herself down on the stage
over and over so hard she leaves bruises all over
her back in ecstasy and thrashes
for the boy who burns the paint off his dorm room walls

She walks fully clothed one April into the midnight cold Pacific
licks salt and honey off the bright god's clavicle
there's a boy who calls her a holy whore
no she never takes money but sometimes thinks why not
it's what I want to do anyway

     It's what I want to do anyway

In a week it will be over
she has stirred her life to the bottom of the pot
tasted those years again when her hair flowed to her shoulders
when any road to any end might run and sometimes did
when her hands shook with the constant cigarettes
there is no happy ending to this drama
but on stage tonight a moment touching his face his hair
gold   red gold   and skin like snow
like sunlight on snow   she steps into the fire

Facing the Audience

Tonight the sea of faces an arm's-length
away as Trinket goes into her tremor
in front of the park bench, and she wants
to be a seagull, raucous, screaming,
she'll eat any trash, Trinket doesn't give a shit
if you see her come. How these kids
parade their bodies. My Celeste lies right down
in the green room, skirt to her hips, thighs spread,
guys watching or playing cards or eating
their takeout Taco Bell, and goes into her
aah-aah-aah-aaah relaxation quiver,
body trembling, pelvis pounding. Oh how
we want to be loved, my mother would drive
eight hours to Claremont to see me act
for an audience of thirteen in some
pretentious play, and tell me then, *you were perfect.*

Aporia

Her thighs through the slit of red kimono
glimmer and shift on the ghostly iron
bedstead. Outside the tattered lace curtain
rain falls, still, rain, as she arches a foot
back and forth, idly, flexing, extending
her toes with their pearly pink nails in time
with Bing Crosby on the radio, "White
Christmas," though here on the streets the sailors
stagger and weave toward the Café Bohème
as she lounges, smoke rising, a single
cigarette. The god has taken her breast.
Carve her shame on the walls, still the question
remains, what space for the sacred
in this century? The actress playing
Trinket, the aging woman whose fingers
never stop moving over the bedposts,
the chenille, who cannot draw hard enough
on the stage non-nicotine cigarette,
her warm breast fills her hand every time her
hand flies to her chest to mark its absence.
So what is missing, after all? Well, what
if the shut door opened in this seedy
New Orleans hotel room, what if the womb
of the actress playing Trinket blossomed
again because the bright god entered,
Mardi Gras beads dropping from her stunned hands?

Gel Room

*Above the main stage, on the way to Trinket's
bedroom, the gel room contains colored plastic sheets
to put over lights. It's a place of transformations.*

Better check my ass in the mirror
to know what they'd see if they were looking—
the guys in the gel room where I change
from patio pants to silk kimono—
the dresser Eric, the Pious Queen, Death
as Jack in Black, and two drunk Sailors.
Never worn a thong in my life.
So I'm stripping down for the undergrads
who turn to watch the walls as I fumble
with pink silk tap pants, camisole, my ankle
slave chain breaks again, and here I am, white
cheeks I hope to God are firm enough
to please these boys if they notice, rushing
to Trinket's room to be abused again.
I'm old enough to be my Sailor's grandma.
But when this boy who will never be my lover—
when he slumps against me drunk just before we
stagger into the bedroom for the sex scene—
well I lean into him then.
We barely speak in the green room,
but once he's Slim who will hurt me, and I'm
Trinket who will flaunt for him, press her
whole body against him—I take comfort
from him then, this 21-year-old
Texan with a brother named Millennius
and another brother named Felix,
I lean into his warm armpit and ribcage
with the trust of the long married.

Trinket's Brag

Bruno: "Ever done it in an alley?"

No but Trinket's done it
        In her mother Mary's bed
                On her mother Julie's floor
    In front of her mother Francesca's full-length mirror

        At the Rodeo Drive-in in Albuquerque
            In Marilee's bunk in Savannah
With Natalie's brother and sister in Santa Fe

On the sand at Coral Gables
              On the stones by Dana Point

Trinket's done it screaming   Laughing   She's done it
   So tenderly   You could set the rain
      And a baby's heartbeat by it

        Trinket's done it
With the Mayor and the President of the International Trade Mart

With a collie   A candle   A pinecone
     Done it burning   Bored   Bleeding

Done it when she knew it was right and done it
        When she knew it was wrong

Done it with her five strong fingers

        With her Father in a dream once
     Lucent he came to her
           Through the valley of ash

With her one and one and one and one and yet again one true love and more

And sometimes Trinket's gone down
>To the river of men
>>And lain on her pallet in rags or naked
>>>Then the bright gods and
>Cockroaches
>>Flowed through her door

Speaking These Lines

*Trinket: "He will be beautiful! Perfect! —Perhaps he'll be
kind, even, so kind I can tell him about my—mutilation."*

Speaking these lines, don't look toward the audience.
Say them on your knees, face the wall above the bar
where stagehands have painted a field of stars,
a galaxy; say them into the whirling field of fire
where stagehands have laid their handprints also,
blue, white, golden, double handprints like birds; say them
into this black, stained and scarred field of paint where human labor
hammers and planes and nails its sets together, look closely.
The coffee is not coffee, wine is not wine—but the wafers
are wafers, and smoke really does rise from the avid ritual,
the mouth and fingers dance that is your Scene One cigarette.
Say these lines which are foolish, which are the heart's
nakedness, proudly, as if the galaxy also whirled
and kindled through your own scarred, stained darkness.

Who Will Be the Richest? Who Will Love Me Most? Who Will Make Me Speak His Name in Tongues?

I ache for you when you're not near but do not tell
anyone about you
        La vida es sueño
    My death prepares in me
                    like the bloodspot of an egg
      and the heart begs for anything but mercy
Piques   Carreaux   Trèfles   Coeurs
             my Sailor laid the cards out
      laid the cards out
          each suit an old lover—

Tell the truth   Once
               I sat all night in the California June
      with just the screen door shut, listening
   to the crickets in the lemon
              tree outside
      the bamboo creaking with growing
I read my book in the shadows
           cast by the single lamp
     nested in a swarm
       of shadows—

Till you came
           arching my spine, making my
     elbows, collarbone, hipbones, taut with warning
   You came to where the
             screen door was shut, locked
    and then you were inside
like turning a glove
          inside out the moment you
    finally make inside outside
      cleanly.

Small Interlude Where She Argues

So easily shamed, aren't we, Trinket?
Women our age, how happy they sometimes
say they are to pass beyond desire, wombs
and breasts like docile children, they learn Greek,
climb mountains. And I think ho ho I'm lost,
the jutting cheekbones, warm flat muscular
body of this boy, beauty like my sons' friends
when they're here on vacation and sleeping, all
ribs and hairy knees and sloping shoulderblades…

Hang on to the real, I tell myself,
meaning, *I know who I am*—

            But Trinket,
when you're kneeling, his hand knotting your hair
as you gaze up at him pretending
he didn't really mean to spill the coffee—
when you're wiping it up then caressing
his ankle, his calf, as he tightens his grip
to force your head back—you know if you could
see yourself you'd cringe, you'd sicken, hunger
so raw in that visibly sagging jawline,
gaunt throat, those veined, trembling fingers.

You want the god to lift you up, don't you—
to forgive you the raddled flesh you can't help
wrapping like mangy furs around the queen self?

Small Interlude, Still, Where She Argues

Hang on to the real, she said to herself,
this is getting full of gods and Sailors.

You can't just admit they're college kids,
you're an English professor and mother of five
slumming in satin, fake fur, and grease paint?

          But gods and Sailors have ribs
and sloping shoulderblades. You cannot know
the blessed ones except in mortal flesh
with mortal longing. Say Christ like any
long-haired friend of your sons walked into the room,
would you fall to your knees or ask Him
to help you change the unreachable light bulb?
Say Beth Ann, commenting on the play,
refers to "the pointy-headed boy who was so mean
to Trinket," and suddenly you see yourselves
with these undazzled eyes, does that make you
any the less Trinket,
or him any the less Trinket's Sailor?

Of Trinket, of Mary

When you stand by the radio after
the Sailor spurns you, and because it is
silent, the cathedral empty, you know
the Christ child has been born, your hand wanders
to that absence as if He seeks the thin blue
milk, the veined orb beneath the cloth of stars—
As your Sailor sleeps his brutal sleep you speak
of the Christ child, his blind sweet hands
fumbling beneath the robes of his mother,
and Trinket, I had that. Rocking or
in bed, or carrying my babies beneath
my pink *ruana* as I walked hours
and hours through the summer woods, their lips
pulling down the starry river, I had that.

Shore Leave

In her dream he flings the cards into a furl,
a flash of light on plum-purple wings
across the high white room where she has just
finished sleeping, finished dreaming of the ocean's
doom and dazzle. He flings the cards out,
swooping, rising, then catches them
into a waterfall. Oh she is young again.
Years spray like mist from his spinning fingers.

But the sea road is his, hers the red gold memory
of his cheek beneath her ring-decked fingers.
In this room at the top of the stairs
where the sad mattress blanches and wakes
beneath the one-breasted moon,
she has only the boys' choir on the radio,
only the candles, the contingencies of roses,
and Mardi Gras beads looped over the mirror.

There Is a Diary Open to the Words

Forgive me.

> I gather a solitary terror around me
> the way you draw together the scarlet
> kimono, wrapping the smooth embroidered
> panels tight across your breast, and then stoop
> to the mirror, unwrapping one side,
> the heart side, just enough to see the pink
> silk camisole. Is there damage there?

> Trinket,
> you've become my dance, today I cannot
> go forward, last night when Arlene wanted
> to do my makeup I just stood there weeping,
> tears making me rivers of soot and green.

"These Our Actors, As I Foretold You"

So Kat fell in love at First Dress with a guy
in the tech room. Now she's radiant but
she can't pee, we used to call it Honeymoon
Fever. Wistaria thickens today
above the porch swing, and dust trails its furry
feet along my unswept floorboards.
The play is over, the scene struck. The Pious
Queen has lost his tiara. My Sailor's
gone off to his girlfriend in Texas.
Priscilla who traced her nipples and howled
like a banshee whore in Scene Four is back
at Blue Marlin waiting tables. Actors
break our hearts, they rejoice in the bright
world in their hands then watch it vanish.
I want life to be kind to them, my *compadres*
and *comadres* at Tennessee Williams's
Silver Dollar Hotel, these kids who flaunt
and flame, who do not sleep, these angels
and divas who belt it out in the green room,
mocking the words to every love song.
While I've been dazzled my yard's sprung up
with colt's-foot, clover. And Trinket's alone
in her room once more, fiddling with the dials,
trying to raise a station on the radio…

It Was Like Being Alive Twice

Now, heart, it is time to be quiet.
The voices have other work to do, someone needs them—

A woman in Great Falls, perhaps,
a blue-haired woman turning round and round
in the calm of her life
while blackbirds rise from shorn wheat fields,
touching her throat with shaking fingers—

All girls who rock themselves on dorm room beds—

A young mother in Metairie. She stirs spaghetti sauce,
diapers her babies, still and always grieving
her Sailor lover's death—
            Suddenly he comes one final time.
The air
grows tight and hot above her shoulders.

Hardest of all to say
            Yes

Hardest of all not to fall on her knees—
To say *Go since you must go, I carry you always.*
I know that you have been here.

Blesser. (Fr.) To Wound, to Hurt; To Offend, to Injure; to Wring, to Shock, to Gall

If *to wound* is *to bless* they are blessed,
Trinket and Celeste, these two drunk, aging floozies—
one needs makeup to look aging and the other,
the desperate courage of aging to play a floozy—
they are blessed as they kneel there with the gallon
jug of Tokay, the crystal wine decanter, and their
loss-induced vision of the Virgin Mary. Oh I know
it's false etymology but think about it: doesn't what
brings you to your knees gut-punched, or makes you
sit on the toilet as your lover lies sleeping
and scratch bright welts along your thighs
with the paring knife, the fingernail scissors,
or drops you fetal to the forest floor because you've
run so far away from home, sobbing *mother, father,*
help me—doesn't the day you stand in the empty house
of the family you destroyed, sent your children
like dandelion seedpods spinning off into the golden
canyons of grief far beyond their small as yet imaginings—
doesn't even this somehow bless them, bless you?
Hard to speak of, even now. You will pray the kind
earth to swallow you.
       Ah, but the god doesn't care.
Trinket turns to the Virgin when the bright one
spurns her. As for you—
that long-ago April you kindled like leaf fire.

"Sonoma Valley" by Crabtree & Evelyn

We've taken the furniture, porcelain,
jewelry, everything but your photographs
and little crystal Buddha. Still you lie there,
lie there. And I pray for your release
from the tyranny of seasons. You open your eyes,
the nurse spoons liquids, but you don't move,
no blink or whisper, like some bivalve
you just shut down more tightly.
        Mother, love, by now your dying
bores me. And for this I think you'd hate me.
Off I've gone to play dress-up with the kids,
to dream about sex and the raunchier angels—
I want sweetness. Didn't you? I want lyrical notes
of "Sonoma Valley," hours and hours
in a honeyed torpor when every petal opens
and opens—or as, on Friday night,
just before the Sailor turned on her forever,
Trinket raked his cheek with peony-lacquered
fingers, wishing she dared rip sweet scarlet berries
from the bone branch, pack her nails with bright
flesh dirt. So I sprayed the cologne I took from you
on the female roués and denizens of the Café
Bohème, the Silver Dollar—on Tiger, Celeste,
The Woman at the Bar—copiously every night
I sprayed your cologne all over my own wrists,
throat, hair, my Trinket breasts, in our good-show-
feel-hot-girls ritual, because we may come
to where you are but for now the shapes
still shift for us, blood still rises in our gorges,
and Tiger who seems shy, a little lonely,
would glance every night at the empty makeup shelf
in the green room and pantomime joy, spreading
her arms out wide like a beauty queen, punching up
the Southern accent, *Why thank you so much.*
You brought me the most beautiful delicious flowahs.

Answers to April

Every year since childhood your piercing greens
stir my heart, constrict the bone
cage of my throat, you flaunt the tenderness
that troubles me in his touch her touch his touch
redbuds sprung to their branches
like blossoms of fever.

Grackles lift and sink
above the broken-shingled roof of my drunk neighbour
where all rots and teems and swells, derelict, dies
and blossoms and I want to too
just cast off this skin, molt, all raw and moist
oh look at the aging woman
dreaming about the cheekbones of boys
April you are shaming me.

You do not grow old in me
your cruelty does not abate
they tell me past the change we grow serene
but the moon still pulls the milky tilth of me
I blush flush
like the petals of dogwoods
opening out today all over town
from wooden to sexual, each with its bite or burn
blessing it
with the mark of its corruption yes yes
I would not be carried
unmarred untorn to the river.

Point Reyes

1

The grey ghost rises on the wind,
splitting the air with his harrying cry.
Great blue herons stalk the tule marshes.
Already, fog gathers on the waters.
It will swell to a spill along Inverness Ridge,
the houses across the water will disappear,
even our own feet will grow cold
and shadowy beneath us. We are spume
on a single wave, a wave that comes to shore
between one foghorn and the next,
and Trinket knows this, that's why she wants
the Sailor, she dreams he will have the roll of the sea
in his thighs, the forgetfulness
of the sea behind his eyes, in his fingers.

2

You whose fingers on this white page
trace their blue scratches and loops in a language
called English, writing where the fog
thickens and rolls in, blotting out the sun
across the mesa   You in whom darkness
flows through all your organs and bones
and just beyond your eyes, beneath the infinite
skin of the world   You whose hand, here
with its two moonstone thumb rings,
its crackly warm terrain of skin and knuckles
and tendons, its pink polished fingernails,
is a moment's stiff or agile knot
of bones and flesh and *prana*   Even now,
as three geese in formation fly overhead
and mist or small rain begins to fall

on the last single-petalled crimson roses,
you move from beauty into beauty.

3

The cricket laps at the night like a cat laps cream.
Grains and knots of this burnished desk wood
flow like the rivers of sand at Limantour Beach,
where I saw a man with feathers, once.
I'd broken away from the boy who tried to kiss me
in the dunes, and walked on down the beach
far from the hot dogs and lemonade.
The man with feathers was dancing, this was 1963.
He croaked and warbled, slowly spiralling up,
up, up, his scrawny arms and fingers
stretching out so wide he held the sky. He scared me.
But I wish I'd gone to sit near him, to watch him
as I idly stroked the warm driftwood, the long
bulbous sea kelp that lay in the luminous sand—
or rise to my feet and begin to dance with him.

Butoh: "Bird"

How silly you are, Trinket. The world
is infinite. Leave your room by the spiral
staircase, leave the ghostly bedstead and
the half-smoked cigarette, Mardi Gras beads
iridescent, gold, blue as the veins of
your hands, on the mirror. Take your scar—
what poets call the proud flesh. Wear it.
Pain is infinite.
                In the Grove
during yoga today, Michele taught us "The Bird,"
a butoh dance move. Mouth opened, eyes closed,
spring's first grass and dogwoods all around her,
her body twisted, spine extended, arm-
wings stiffened, rose slowly, slowly, till she
clawed frozen at heaven—then sank down
into the egg again, rested there, grass-washed,
sun-licked. Watching, I thought, that's *your* dance,
Trinket, when you spasm by the park bench,
when your mouth opens but no sound comes out,
that rictus and writhe, wild with the bitter-old
winter-cold hunger for love—that "Bird,"
dance form born of the dying—

Acknowledgements

"Aporia" was first published in *Center*. "After Many Years She Returns to the Stage in a Play by Tennessee Williams," "Trinket's Brag," and "*Blesser.* (Fr.) To Wound, to Hurt; to Offend, to Injure; to Wring, To Shock, to Gall" were first published in *Flyway*.

"These Our Actors, As I Foretold You":

Prospero:

> Our revels now are ended. These our actors,
> As I foretold you, were all spirits and
> Are melted into air, into thin air:
> And, like the baseless fabric of this vision,
> The cloud-capp'd towers, the gorgeous palaces,
> The solemn temples, the great globe itself,
> Yea, all which it inherit, shall dissolve
> And, like this insubstantial pageant faded,
> Leave not a rack behind. We are such stuff
> As dreams are made on, and our little life
> Is rounded with a sleep.
>   (The Tempest IV. i)

"Sonoma Valley" by Crabtree & Evelyn:

"Sonoma Valley" is a cologne fragrance created by the company Crabtree & Evelyn.

Ann Fisher-Wirth is Professor of English at the University of
Mississippi. In 2002-2003 she holds the Fulbright Distinguished Chair
of American Studies at Uppsala University, Sweden.

She is the author of *Blue Window*, published by Archer Books in 2003.

Dana Sonnenschein received her B.A. from the University of Iowa, an M.A. in poetry from The Writing Seminars, Johns Hopkins University, and an M.A. and Ph.D. in literature from Boston University. At present, she is an associate professor of English at Southern Connecticut State University in New Haven, and she and her husband live in nearby Bethany, on the edge of the Naugatuck State Forest.

Her poetry has appeared in *Amazing Stories, Appalachia, Blueline, Calapooya, the Connecticut Review, The Hogtown Creek Review, The Indiana Review, The Iowa Review, The Northwest Review, Passages North, The Spoon River Poetry Review, Writer's Forum,* and other journals.

ACKNOWLEDGEMENTS

"Cemetery Angel" was first published in *Calapooya* and "Shadow of a Shadow" in the *Hogtown Creek Review*. "In the North Woods," "How Can You Tell a Raven from a Crow?" and "*Corvus corax* at the White Tower" have been accepted at *Heaven Bone*.

"Raven Songs" are translated from Fr. Klaeber's Old English edition of *Beowulf and the Fight at Finnsburg*, (Lexington, MA: D.C. Heath, 1950). The raven behavior in "Raven Games" and "On Natural Selection" is reported in Bernd Heinrich's *Mind of the Raven* (New York: HarperCollins, 1999). The crow tale and history of corn in "Indian Giver" are drawn from displays in the Mashantucket Pequot Museum and Research Center. "The Cursing of the Birds" is based on the Ila tale of the same name, appearing in *African Folktales*, selected and retold by Roger D. Abrahams (New York: Pantheon, 1983). "Wall of the Crow" is informed by recent research reported in "The Pyramid Builders," *National Geographic* 200.5 (November 2001): 78-99, and in *Ancient Egypt*, edited by David P. Silverman (New York: Oxford University Press, 1997). Finally, the Japanese conception of the sun as a red crow referred to in "Ideogram" and the rhymes in "Crow Calling" were collected by Laura C. Martin and appear in her *Folklore of Birds* (Old Saybrook, CT: Globe Pequot Press, 1993).